Fostering Diversity, Equity, and Inclusion in the Workplace

Workbook

A Competency-Based Approach to Understanding and Fostering Diversity, Equity, and Inclusion in the Workplace

First Edition 2022

ISBN: 9798794743647

Centrestar Learning
State College, Pennsylvania, USA
www.centrestar.com

Fostering Diversity, Equity, and Inclusion in the Workplace

Endorsements for Dr. Wesley Donahue's Fostering Diversity, Equity, and Inclusion in the Workplace

"In his workbook, Fostering Diversity, Equity, and Inclusion in the Workplace, Dr. Donahue provides very pertinent and valuable leadership lessons that is an absolute must read for current and aspiring leaders. The key concepts that are addressed in the workbook provide essential foundational knowledge of diversity and inclusion to strengthen interpersonal relationships and build core leadership competencies."

— Nikhil Juneja,
MBA, Program Quality Manager, General Motors

"Wow! Wes Donahue has dealt most effectively with a tough topic--diversity. If you want a skill building treatment on this topic--and you should want that--then this book is it. It is well worth buying, reading--and using."

— William J. Rothwell,
Ph.D., SPHR, SHRM-SCP, RODC, CPLP Fellow, President, Rothwell & Associates, Inc. & LLC and Professor, Workforce Education & Development, Penn State University, University Park

"Diversity, Equity, and Inclusion (DE&I) is a focus that organizations are dedicating the time, energy and resources needed to impact their organizational ecosystem and increase the feeling of belonging among employees and stakeholders. Dr. Donahue has created a practical yet simple workbook and "must read" guide for individuals and leaders at all levels ready to foster an organizational shift of embedding DE&I into their organizational DNA. Additionally, this book is a terrific resource for internal and external seminars, workshops, and lunch-and-learn programs."

— Leila Farzam,
Ph.D., Subject Matter Expert | Advisory Services Practice, REI Systems, Inc.

"While others are struggling to understand DEI, Dr. Donahue puts it into plain English with actionable steps to improve organizational efforts and understanding. This is a great addition to any organization's learning curriculum. "

— Phillip L. Ealy,
M.P.S., CYFAR PDTA Center Coaching Coordinator, Implementation Specialist Clearinghouse for Military Family Readiness, The Pennsylvania State University

"If you care deeply about organizational diversity and its benefit accompanied with inclusive organizational culture, then put this book on your required-reading list. You will learn theoretical knowledge and practical skills of how you can create diverse and inclusive organization."

— Bora Kwon,
Ph.D., Assistant Professor of Management, Jack Welch College of Business and Technology at Sacred Heart University

"Great book! I really liked how this book emphasized the value of diversity in the workplace. It truly provides a multitude of benefits for employees, employers, and the organization as a whole. The book introduced protocols that can be established at the workplace. I think this is a nice approach that allows transparency and equity. Also, the book talked about how we could reexamine our own biases even if they are subconscious. Not only did I learn a lot of knowledge about diversity and interpersonal relationships, but I also have developed many new perspectives of diversity."

— Aura Zhao,
Quality Manager, Bakery Barn LLC, Pleasant Hills, PA

"Fostering Diversity, Equity, and Inclusion in the Workplace is a workbook in which Professor Donahue uses his work background managing projects for a U.S. organization that was among the 500 Fortune companies, in addition to his scholarly experience at the Pennsylvania State University. I found this book is invaluable for organization diversity, inclusion, and equity officers and the top echelon in guiding their effort to foster diversity and inclusion more effectively. This workbook could help workplace learning professionals to develop competencies and behaviors by identifying their needs and areas of improvement in promoting diversity, equity, and Inclusion in the Workplace."

— Abdelfatah Arman,
Ph.D., Assistant Professor, School of Business Administration, American University of Ras Al Khaimah, United Arab Emirates

"Today's work organizations have increasingly diverse workforces, and many leaders aren't sure about how to manage this diversity. This *Fostering Diversity, Equity, and Inclusion in the Workplace* workbook offers much needed positive and practical tools to help employees—and supervisors— contribute to work environments where diversity is considered a strength and all organizational members feel valued and included."

— Katheryn K. Woodley,
Ph.D., Industrial-Organizational psychologist; retired Penn State Management Development faculty member with over 30 years of experience in leadership development

Fostering Diversity, Equity, and Inclusion in the Workplace
Workbook

A Competency-Based Approach to Understanding and Fostering Diversity, Equity, and Inclusion in the Workplace

Diversity is the one thing we all have in common. Celebrate it every day.

— Winston Churchill

Preface

There are a couple of things that I have learned over my career which have been reinforced by my global business travels. First, human beings have pretty much the same needs the world around, and second, the "Golden Rule" of treating others as you would like others to treat you applies now more than ever.

However, many times, people are lumped into groups and stereotyped by age, religion, race, gender, ethnicity, etc. And while such groups may have common history and traits it can be a mistake to stereotype them all as being the same. Not all men like sports, not all baby boomers are workaholics, and I suspect that not all French are good lovers. However, we are all unique individuals with our experiences and perspectives on life and work. Our DNA may account for some of our human factor difference, however how we were raised and how we are treated in the environments in which we live, and work can be vastly different, as well.

In some environments, people are still working under a caste system where class structure is determined at birth. In other environments, productivity is paramount and trumps any discussion of work-life balance. And in still other environments family comes first and work is something that you do to help you to achieve something else.

We should all recognize that power differences in most organizations are a reality, fostering team efforts in the workplace takes effort, and promoting diversity, equity, and inclusion is everyone's job in today's multicultural organizations, but their value and benefits to an organization cannot be understated. The overarching objectives of this workbook are to help individuals appreciate cultural protocols, recognize that we are all different, and envision the benefits of fostering diversity, equity, and inclusion in your workplace.

This workbook will also help you build your competence in recognizing and appreciating your own individual differences. The competencies associated with this workbook include: Interpersonal Skills; Interpersonal Relationship Building: and Diverse Workforce.

People working together in diverse and inclusive workplaces can make a positive impact on the individuals, teams, and organizations they serve. As famous American cultural anthropologist, Margret Mead, once said, "Never doubt that a small group of thoughtful, committed, citizens can change the world. Indeed, it is the only thing that ever has."

Dr. Wesley E. Donahue   2022

Acknowledgments

I did not create this workbook alone, and I want to acknowledge the people who contributed significantly to the work: Drs. Lisa Donahue, Rebecca Sarnaski, and Katheryn Woodley for their invaluable research efforts in tracking down articles, books, and other sources needed for content development and identifying examples; Billie Tomlinson for her editing and attention to detail; Valentine Platon for adding graphics that help bring the text to life; Alex Donahue for thoughtful design suggestions; former instructors and professional associates at Penn State Management who shared their business and industry wisdom and years of teaching experience; the individuals who took the time to review the manuscript; and the many thousands of people who participated in surveys, focus groups, and interviews, without whom this workbook would lack the richness of real-world detail. To all these people I offer a sincere and heartfelt Thank you!

A lot of different flowers make a bouquet.

— Islamic Proverb

Structured Learning Design

All our workbooks align with our research-based **Competency Model.** The model, which is rooted in work by the U.S. Department of Labor and others, gives you a framework for structured learning by helping you identify and develop specific competencies.

If you ask people to define competency, you may be amazed at the variety of responses you receive. We define a *competency* as a set of skills, knowledge, attitudes, and behaviors that are observable and measurable. *The emphasis here is on observable and measurable.* It is not enough that you *think* you are competent in an area. You must be able to *behave* in ways that demonstrate your competence to others.

Our framework has **35 competency dimensions** associated with successful performance in leadership and professional roles.

Centrestar Competency Model

Based on thousands of business participant responses from many industries, we clustered these 35 competencies into five competency domains, which we named and coded as follows:

- A. Resource Management
- B. Professional Competence
- C. Supervisory/Management
- D. Organizational Leadership
- E. Technical Acumen

Competencies and clusters may overlap, but for each workbook we identify the three competencies with which the content is most closely associated. Our **Fostering Diversity and Inclusion in the Workplace** workbook focuses on the competency areas of **Interpersonal Skills**, **Interpersonal Relationship Building**, and **Diverse Workforce**. The content is most associated with the **Professional Competence** competency cluster, as shown below.

A. RESOURCE MANAGEMENT
_____ 1. Computer and Literacy Skills
_____ 2. Technical Competence
_____ 3. Resource Usage
_____ 4. Resource Management
_____ 5. Understands Systems

B. PROFESSIONAL COMPETENCE
_____ 6. Conceptual Thinking
_____ 7. Learning and Information Skills
_____ 8. Self-Responsibility and Management
_X___ 9. Interpersonal Skills
_____ 10. Oral Communication
_____ 11. Written Communication

D. ORGANIZATIONAL LEADERSHIP
_____ 22. Human Performance Management
_____ 23. Planning and Evaluation
_____ 24. Financial Management and Budgeting
_____ 25. Technology Management
_____ 26. Creative Thinking
_____ 27. Vision
_____ 28. External Awareness
_____ 29. Strategic Thinking and Planning
_____ 30. Management Controls
_X___ 31. Diverse Workforce
_____ 32. Leading Change

Centrestar Competency Model

C. SUPERVISORY MANAGEMENT
_____ 12. Leadership and Coaching
_____ 13. Flexibility and Resilience
_____ 14. Problem Solving
_____ 15. Decisiveness
_____ 16. Self-Direction
_____ 17. Conflict Management
_____ 18. Teamwork and Cooperation
_____ 19. Influencing and Negotiating
_____ 20. Customer Focus
_X___ 21. Interpersonal Relationship Building

E. TECHNICAL ACUMEN
_____ 33. Job-Specific Competencies
_____ 34. Occupational Competencies
_____ 35. Industry-Wide Competencies

How to Use this Workbook

This workbook is structured to be a hands-on guide with options for how you can use the material.

One way to use the workbook is to read it straight through. Or you can jump to specific sections depending on your interests and goals. We recommend you start by reviewing the table of contents, so you understand the workbook's organization. Read the overview, and then take the introductory assessment by rating your level of agreement with the ten statements. This will help you clarify your current thinking. After that, scan the workbook. Scanning will help you pinpoint areas where you may have an information gap and areas where feel confident. From there, you can set your learning goals and dive deeper into the material.

The workbook will help you develop your competence by addressing the ten most vital concepts associated with a topical area. The content for the ten concepts is structured in a consistent learning format.

Each concept starts with several paragraphs of relevant content and ends with three **What to Do** action suggestions, followed by a **Remember** section which lists important learning points. To **Enhance Your Learning**, we offer links to additional resources. Each concept area concludes with a **Reinforce Your Learning** application activity.

At the end of workbook is a **Summary** and a **Recap Checklist**. The recap lists all the 30 **What to Do** actions from each concept in the workbook.

A 20-question **Knowledge Review Test** is also available with answers. You can use it to test your knowledge, or it is an optional feature for those who seek to earn development hours (4 hrs.) to maintain their professional credentials. For more information about professional development hours, visit our website at www.centrestar.com.

As with most things in life, **you will get out of this workbook only what you put into it.** To learn and grow you must engage fully with the material presented. Ask yourself questions as you read the material in the workbook. Do the activities and answer the questions in each concept? Make notes. Look for ideas new to you and consider how they fit with your current knowledge. Recognize what you already know and can build on, and what might be a new way of looking at something.

This workbook aims to ensure that your skills are at the highest level they can be. Engaging with the concepts and materials will help you become a more rounded professional who experiences success in your chosen career.

An individual has not started living until he can rise above the narrow confines of his individualistic concerns to the broader concerns of all humanity.

— Martin Luther King Jr.

Contents

Our diversity is our strength.
What a dull and pointless life it would be if everyone was the same.

— Angelina Jolie

Overview

We are a nation of communities... a brilliant diversity spread like stars, like a thousand points of light in a broad and peaceful sky.

– George H. W. Bush

Today it is the rare workplace that is not diverse in employees, customers or suppliers, and often in all three. Everyone benefits from the different points of view, knowledge, and experience that people from different communities can bring to an organization. In fact, studies show that organizations with ample diversity in their leadership and workforce are more profitable than those that have little or no diversity.

In this workbook, you will learn about the value of diversity, equity, and inclusion in the workplace. This workbook focuses on appreciating cultural protocols as they relate to the workplace, understanding organizational power differences, improving workplace relationships, mitigating resistance to adopting new beliefs or behaviors, and promoting equity and inclusion in today's multicultural organizations.

By the end of this workbook, you will:

- Recognize the scope and importance of diversity in today's work organizations.
- Gain foundational knowledge of best practices in diversity, equity, and inclusion.
- Be mindful of cultural protocols in the workplace.
- Understand how perceptions can be filtered through unconscious bias.
- Know how to improve workplace relationships.

The competencies and behaviors developed throughout this workbook include:

Interpersonal Skills   **Interpersonal Relationship Building**   **Diverse Workforce**

Take Your Temperature for Fostering Diversity, Equity, and Inclusion in the Workplace

Start to identify what you know about fostering diversity, equity, and inclusion in the workplace and the areas where you can improve. Following is an assessment to help you. With you and your organization in mind, read each statement below and write the number from 1 to 10 that indicates your level of agreement with the statement, with **1** being **strongly disagree** and **10** being **strongly agree**.

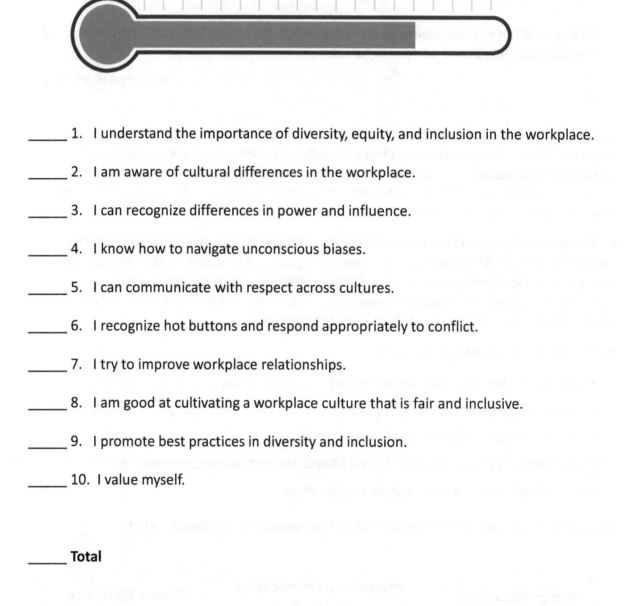

_____ 1. I understand the importance of diversity, equity, and inclusion in the workplace.

_____ 2. I am aware of cultural differences in the workplace.

_____ 3. I can recognize differences in power and influence.

_____ 4. I know how to navigate unconscious biases.

_____ 5. I can communicate with respect across cultures.

_____ 6. I recognize hot buttons and respond appropriately to conflict.

_____ 7. I try to improve workplace relationships.

_____ 8. I am good at cultivating a workplace culture that is fair and inclusive.

_____ 9. I promote best practices in diversity and inclusion.

_____ 10. I value myself.

_____ **Total**

Take a moment to reflect on the following before you move forward in the course:

What is your job? Have you considered how your job relates to your organization's goals and supports its values regarding diversity as well as broader goals and values?

What problems or situations have you experienced or observed related to fostering diversity, equity, and inclusion in the workplace?

Take a few minutes to reflect on your self-assessment. List two or three areas you want to improve.

As you progress through this workbook consider what actions you can take to demonstrate competence in the following three competency areas:

1. **Interpersonal Skills** – appropriately sociable; interacts effectively with others

_____

_____

_____

_____

_____

2. **Interpersonal Relationship Building** – considers and responds appropriately to the needs, feelings, and capabilities of others; seeks feedback and accurately assesses impact on others; provides helpful feedback; builds trust with others

_____

_____

_____

_____

_____

3. **Diverse Workforce** – recognizes the value of culture, ethnic, gender, and other differences; provides employment and development opportunities for a diverse workforce

_____

_____

_____

_____

_____

Understand Diversity, Equity, and Inclusion in the Workplace

Diversity and *inclusion* have become buzzwords in the last couple of decades and are terms used by organizations in marketing, job listings, mission statements, and more. But too often, individuals in the workplace do not understand why diversity and inclusion are important or what the terms mean. They may refer to them in theory but fail to embrace them as tangible and valuable operational concepts. Further, people often confuse the terms equity and equality and use them interchangeability, though they are quite different in meaning. These terms will be defined below.

Diversity is more than a buzzword. It is a workplace necessity. Studies show that organizations who have diversity in their leadership and workforce are more profitable than those who do not. McKinsey studied 180 large publicly traded companies in the United States, United Kingdom, France and Germany and found that those whose senior leadership included women and foreign nationals had up to 53 percent higher returns on equity and 14 percent higher earnings than less diverse organizations (as cited in Joshi, 2018).

Diverse Senior Leadership		**Diverse Board**

Higher returns on equity	Higher earnings	Higher performance

A subsequent study found that organizations with at least one female on their Board of Directors outperformed those with no female Board members by 26 percent (Joshi, 2018).

The evidence from these and other sources is staggering. Diversity is good business.

Here are some things you need to know about diversity and inclusion in the workplace:

Following is some useful terminology adapted from What Does Diversity, Equity and Inclusion (DEI) Mean in the Workplace? (Heinz, 2021), and Terms & Definitions. (Extension Foundation, 2021):

- **Diversity** is the presence of differences within a given setting. It refers to people who bring differences to the workplace, such as different backgrounds, experiences, knowledge, belief systems, and ways of thinking. Different types of diversity include, among other things, race, ethnicity, religious beliefs, age, gender, sexual orientation, physical and intellectual abilities, heritage and socio-economic status (SES).

- **Inclusion** is the practice of ensuring that people feel a sense of belonging in the workplace. An inclusive culture is one in which diversity is treated as a strength that helps the organization innovate, succeed, and survive.

- **Equality** means everyone is treated the same exact way, regardless of need or any other individual difference.

- **Equity** is the process of ensuring that processes and programs are impartial, fair, and provide equal possible outcomes for every individual. The equal possible outcomes recognizes that each person or group may be different, and that unique resources or opportunities may be needed to eliminate barriers. For example, the Americans with Disabilities Act (ADA) was written to ensure equal access to public places.

People sometimes think of embracing diversity as simply making all organizational members feel welcome—a sort of pleasantry. But the reality is, embracing diversity is also about benefiting from the contributions of those organizational members. When we have diverse people in the workforce and in leadership, and support their unique talents and contributions, we widen our understanding of products, services, and customers. We bring new ideas, new ways of looking at problems, and, thus, new solutions to the organization. Diversity brings the potential for organizations to be smarter and stronger, as well offer better environments in which to work.

Most organizations today provide products or services to a broad and diverse customer base, and that customer base is becoming more diverse than ever. Having a workforce that is also diverse can help an organization to better understand its customers (Feigenbaum, 2018).

Here are some of the **benefits** inherent in a diverse workforce (Feigenbaum, 2018):

- **Diversity in language**. People come with different languages but also with different communication skills. "Having someone within your organization who can explain the subtle differences in how cultures view things can be the difference between launching a great campaign and blowing a great opportunity."

- **Diversity in ideas**. Employees from different backgrounds often have different ideas about how to approach product development, marketing, problem-solving, communication, and more. Obtaining views from a wide variety of people can result in a better product or service, and thus more profits and a better standard of living for all.

- **Economic and target-market diversity**. People from different backgrounds will help the organization form a more well-rounded view of various customer markets. For example, many hospitals in U.S. urban areas benefit from having Hispanic and Asian staff members who can communicate to patients who have similar backgrounds. They also have a better understanding of cultural sensitivities, such as the patient's need to have a same-sex nurse or assistant when getting help in the restroom. This can be what gets one hospital better reviews and more business than another.

To further illustrate the value of diverse teams, one study looked at how juries performed in court settings (Joshi, 2018). The researchers found that panels of white and black participants performed better than all-white groups in many measures. "Such diverse juries deliberated longer, raised more facts about the case, and conducted broader and more wide-ranging deliberations... They also made fewer factual errors in discussing evidence and, when errors did occur, those errors were more likely to be corrected during the discussion" (Joshi, 2018).

There are additional benefits from a diverse workforce, (Joshi, 2018):

- "Researchers from Columbia, MIT, University of Texas-Dallas, Northwestern, and a few other prestigious universities looked at stock-picking in ethnically homogenous and diverse groups... The findings of the study revealed that the financial decisions of the more diverse groups were 58 percent better than those of the homogenous groups, which led to fewer bubbles on the market."

- "A study published in *Scientific American* in 2014 looked at 1.5 million academic papers and found that papers written by diverse groups were more likely to receive citations and had higher impact factors than those whose authors belonged to the same ethnic group. They also found that people of similar ethnicities were more likely to collaborate on papers more often, but the final product was much more impactful in the diverse groups."

What to do:

- ☐ Recognize the value of diversity, equity, and inclusion in your workplace.
- ☐ Consider how having diverse leadership and a diverse workforce can benefit your organization.
- ☐ Understand that diversity is more than a buzzword. Diversity is good business.

Other actions:

- ☐ _____
- ☐ _____
- ☐ _____
- ☐ _____
- ☐ _____

Remember

✓ Diversity means including different types of people to open up new ideas within your organization.

✓ Diversity should start at the top and be present at every level. Even if you are not at the top of your organization, you can support a culture that embraces and values diversity.

✓ Studies show that organizations with diverse leadership and workforces are higher performing and more profitable.

Enhance Your Learning

Review the following terms and definitions offered by the Access, Equity, and Belonging Committee of Cooperative Extension unit of the U.S Department of Agriculture.

The Access, Equity, and Belonging: Terms & Definitions. Extension Foundation. (2021)		Available at: https://access-equity-belonging.extension.org/terms-definitions/

Watch the following entertaining and poignant fifteen-minute video about diversity in the workplace. As you watch, ask yourself the question: **how are you diverse from others in your workplace? C**onsider changing the narrative, from everyone else is different and you must accommodate them.

The Surprising Solution to Workplace Diversity. Tedx Talks. Mahdawi, A. (2016)		Available at: https://www.youtube.com/watch?v=mtUIRYXJ0vI

Reinforce Your Learning

My Beliefs. Take a moment to reflect on your beliefs. Answer the following questions:

- Do I see the value of having diversity in leadership in my organization? If so, what are the benefits?

- Do I see the value of having diversity in my work team or group? If so, what value does diversity bring?

- Do I see myself as different from others in my workplace? If so, how are you different and what value does it bring?

- Do I see any barriers to embracing diversity in my organization? If so, what can be done to remove those barriers?

"Our ability to reach unity in diversity will be the beauty and the test of our civilization."

— Mahatma Gandhi

Be Aware of Culture in Work Relationships

In the world of today, we interact with people from other cultures more than ever before. We travel more, communicate via social media, see world news on our local news channels, sell to customers in other countries, buy from people in other countries, and interact with colleagues, leaders, suppliers, and customers from around the world.

The interaction is exciting in many ways and there is much to gain from working across different cultures. However, there can be challenges, such as uncertainty about how to behave when we interact with people from other cultures. For example, should you attempt to form a personal connection or keep everything strictly professional? Luckily, there are many online and educational sources that can be accessed to provide needed information. When you expect to interact with people from a culture with which you are unfamiliar, you can reduce your uncertainty and improve the chances of a positive interaction if you do a bit of cultural research beforehand.

Most organizations in the US follow predominantly Western cultural traditions. For those raised in this culture, they tend to behave in concert with its traditions without giving it too much thought. But people from different cultures have to think more deeply about how to behave. Sometimes, they may lose some of their uniqueness as they attempt to adapt to more Western traditions. However, as "westerners" we must realize that differences exist from region to region. For example, consider the cultural differences of the U.S. Northeast, South, Southwest, Midwest, etc. Differences such as food preferences, language dialects, dress habits, etc. are apparent. There is value in learning from different cultures, rather than expecting others to conform to our unique individual protocols.

Here is what you need to know about cultural protocols:

The term *cultural protocols* refers to the customs, actions, codes, ethics, and behaviors that guide people of a particular cultural group. As an individual, you have your own cultural protocols. These include most of the things you do in life, from: how you greet a relative to how you greet a person you just met; the holidays you celebrate; the kinds of foods you eat; and even the words you use when you are angry. Some of these you likely share with other members of your cultural group. But even though you share a cultural heritage with others, you are still unique.

- Every person is unique. Learning about another culture will help you better understand people in that culture, but you still need to treat each person as a unique individual.

- There is a difference between understanding a person's cultural heritage and stereotyping that person.

While respecting that each individual is different, understanding that people have beliefs and behaviors that stem from their heritage will help you build work relationships with people. It is important that we all try to understand our own differences as well as the cultural similarities and differences of the people with whom we work. Acknowledging and respecting cultural traditions can mean the difference between having effective working relationships and not being able to get things done.

One way to understand the impact that cultural differences might have on work relationships is to consider differences in basic values. While different models use somewhat different language and categories, the following nine illustrate the primary differences that are seen at a national level (Include-Empower, 2015):

1. **Individualism vs. Collectivism.** Is the focus on "I" or "we," on individual goals or group welfare?

2. **Power Distance**. This refers to the spread of power within a group and is covered in more depth in Concept 3.

3. **Uncertainty Avoidance.** Are members more comfortable with change and risk taking or with predictability and following the rules?

4. **Orientation to Time**. Is the focus on the future—long term goals, delayed gratification—or on the present, instant gratification?

5. **Gender Egalitarianism**. Are the characteristics, organizational roles and status accorded to men and women similar or very different?

6. **Assertiveness**. What is valued more: strength, competition and success or tenderness, modesty and cooperation?

7. **Being vs. Doing**. Is there a preference for changing the world to fit the individual (doing) or for the individual to find ways to fit into the world as it is (being)?

8. **Humane Orientation**. Is there a sense of responsibility for the well-being of others?

9. **Indulgence vs. Restraint**. Does the society encourage or discourage pleasure-seeking behavior.

Any of these values, or any combination of them, can translate to differences in the behaviors and expectations of people who work together. They can affect willingness to participate in a team, acceptance of personal or individual credit, openness in expressing opinions or disagreeing with another person's opinion, willingness to give corrective feedback, comfort in reporting to a female manager, how rigorously the workday should be scheduled, the types of work goals that are seen as most important, and what our responsibilities are for dealing with racial or other forms of discriminatory behavior or practices.

Simply reflecting on these differing values should help you better understand some of the reasons why building productive work relationships in culturally diverse groups can be challenging. However, it is a mistake to assume that everyone raised in a country having a particular set of values is identical to everyone else.

Beyond national differences, there are cultural differences resulting from the region of the country where someone grew up, their religion, their age (generational group), and whether they were raised in an urban, suburban or rural setting. These differences increase the importance of remembering that, while people with the same national background share some beliefs and preferences, they are not identical.

Today, there are more **generational groups** in the workplace than ever before. Millennials work alongside those from GenX, as well as Baby Boomers and even a few Traditionalist or GI Generation members. Members in each group will share influences that affect their behaviors and characteristics common to their age group. Understanding these differences can improve communication and working relationships.

Besides acknowledging and respecting differences among people, be aware of your beliefs. When it comes to working with others, start by assessing your preconceived ideas.

Here are some typical categories that will help you assess your ideas about others:

- First, some people have prejudices that are obvious and openly expressed. Their negativity and distrust may be expressed against the members of one or more groups of people who are different from them. Often their prejudices are deep-seated beliefs, developed out of fear and lack of understanding. It can be difficult for them to change their beliefs.

- Second, some people have minor prejudices they learned as children, but they try not to let them interfere with how they treat others at work. While these people typically do not demonstrate their prejudices publicly, they may express their beliefs openly when at home. People in this category, if motivated to do so, can learn to get past their prejudices and value diversity. On the other hand, because they are reinforcing their prejudiced beliefs in private, they could begin to express their beliefs in more public settings. How people speak and behave in private becomes part of their thought process. For them to overcome prejudices, they must first change how they think.

- Third, some people may have been raised with some prejudices but, for the most part, they believe in treating all people fairly and equitably. People in this group can, however, have some biases of which they are not aware. For example, someone with this type of bias may quickly lock the car door as soon as they start to drive through a community dominated by people whose skin color is different from theirs. Or if walking, they may clutch their bag or briefcase a little tighter. They do not think they have a bias, but they do. To move closer to embracing diversity, they need to recognize and deal with their unconscious bias.

- Finally, some people were either raised, or learned for themselves, to value diversity and treat all people equitably. Even someone in this group may have a situational bias of which they are unaware and may need to bring the bias to conscious awareness in order not to act on it.

In short, everyone is susceptible to bias or prejudice: We all may have some work to do! Whichever group you fall into, your immediate goal should be to understand what constitutes prejudicial or biased treatment, and to exhibit as little of these behaviors as possible in working with others. Your longer-term goal should be to purge bias and prejudice against people from your thoughts and beliefs, so that you are behaving authentically. Having consistency between your thoughts and actions increases your effectiveness in forging productive and positive relationships with others, and is also more gratifying to you.

Start by recognizing that what you think is incorrect behavior might be a cultural belief. For example: "Different cultures also have different ideas about time. In the United States, an appointment is a time someone is expected to arrive. In some countries, an appointment is the earliest someone is expected to arrive, but they could arrive much later. Individuals in the global workplace should appreciate and accommodate these cultural differences" (Lumen, n.d.).

Your perceptions are filtered through your cultural beliefs, experiences, and unconscious biases. It is up to you to consider your assumptions and to work to understand what is really happening when you interpret another person's behavior.

What to do:	Other actions:
☐ Pay attention to people around you and be aware of differences and similarities.	☐ _____ ☐ _____
☐ Recognize how you are different and be mindful of your behavior.	☐ _____ ☐ _____
☐ Make an effort to understand and value the people with whom you work.	☐ _____

Remember

✓ Every person is unique. Teams made up of people with different experiences, backgrounds, and knowledge tend to perform better than those with less diversity.

✓ Anger and prejudice often come from fear. Work to understand people who are different from you, so you can overcome fear and any prejudices you have.

✓ Resist the temptation to expect everyone to "Americanize." For example, many people from Asian countries have started shaking hands when greeting Americans, even though many of them prefer to bow. Do not be offended if they bow instead of shaking hands.

✓ Be mindful of people's beliefs and cultural protocols as they relate to the workplace. Shaking hands, making eye contact, and taking Christmas vacation may be important to some people, but other people may not hold those actions in the same regard.

Enhance Your Learning

Here is an example from Apple about truly valuing lives. Watch this two-minute video and check out their diversity video below. Consider how you can apply this information in your work:

Apple – Inclusion & Diversity – Open. Apple. (2017)		Available at: https://www.youtube.com/watch?v=cvb49-Csq1o

Watch this fifteen-minute TEDxCreightonU video to lean more about generational differences and today's multigenerational workplace.

Navigating the Multigenerational Workplace. (2018)		Available at: https://www.youtube.com/watch?v=kzfAOc4L6vQ

Reinforce your learning

Generations in Your Workplace. Which generations are currently in your workplace? Check those that are present, then **describe events** or **influences** on each that may have an effect on each generation's work behaviors, attitudes, or characteristics. Note that dates used to define each generation are approximate; and some people's experiences may be more reflective of a preceding or succeeding generation..

- **Traditionalists**
  (Born 1925 – 1946, now in their 70s, 80s and 90's; Also called the Silent Generation):

- **Baby Boomers** (Born 1947 – 1963, now in their upper-50s to early 70's):

- **Generation X** (Born 1964 – 1983, in their upper-30s to upper-50s):

- **Millennials** (Born 1984 – 1996, in their mid-20s to upper-30s; Also called Generation Y):

- **Generation Z** (Born 1997 and beyond, mostly low-20's and under; Also called the Post 9/11 Generation, Centennials, and Post-Millennials):

Consider Differences in Power and Influence

Individuals differ in how they perceive and use power and it is easy to overlook, or minimize, the problems that result from perceptions about power, and who has it and who does not.

Power is a fascinating thing. They say that absolute power corrupts absolutely, and when a person has a taste for power, they want more. Power makes us feel stronger, better, and that we are important. But that doesn't mean that power is inherently good or bad. In reality, we all need some form of power to thrive, so in that sense, it is good. However, power does become problematic, or bad, when it is used to take advantage of others or to deny them access to things they have a legitimate right to have.

Everyone has some type of power. As individuals in the workplace, we have influence over others, at least to some extent. But, from where does power or influence come? Why do you have it, and how do you use it? A currently popular theory about power is an expansion of the classic work of French and Raven (1959), who looked at power as deriving from five sources, or bases. Two other bases were added later, which resulted in the following seven:

- **Legitimate power**. This is the power of position or title. Within the legitimate range of your responsibilities, you can ask people to comply with your requests just because you have the organizationally-conferred right to do so. Being a team leader gives you an element of control over people, but does not guarantee that they will comply.

- **Reward Power**. This power comes from your ability to provide rewards that people value, such as approving assignments, influencing raises, or recognizing their ideas and contributions.

- **Coercive Power**. This is the power of threat. When you have coercive power, you are perceived as being able to inflict something painful if those you are trying to influence do not comply. People respond to your requests out of fear of punishment.

- **Expert Power**. This is the power of expert knowledge. You can influence others to support your ideas and causes because they respect your knowledge, skills and understanding of an issue. They go along because they trust your expertise.

- **Referent Power**. This is the power of personal appeal. You are able to influence others to support you because they like you, want to be like you, want your respect, or don't want to cause you problems. This power comes from your personal characteristics, personality, charisma, integrity, or reputation of accomplishments.

- **Information Power**. If you have this power base, others may comply because you have access to information they need or that is perceived as important to them, which they cannot access on their own.

- **Connection Power**. This is the power of "who you know." The ability to influence derives not from your personal ability to offer rewards or exact threats, but rather from your connections with influential or important people who do have that capability, or who others would want to please.

Inequalities Among Groups. One way to consider the ramifications of power in the workplace is to observe the inequalities among groups of people and individuals. That is, certain groups may have more power, while other groups have less, or have difficulty asserting their power and being taken seriously. For example, in some workplaces, women have less power as compared to men, and power differences can be based on heritage or demographics.

In many ways, history is about power differences, both real and perceived. For example, in our time, some groups may seem to feel they do not have, or are losing power, while others may feel they are gaining power. Regardless of what is happening in any group or society at any particular time, a better understanding of power is useful for everyone.

As a society, we have tried to deal with power inequalities in multiple ways, from affirmative action and hiring quotas to ADA compliance laws. We have come a long way in raising awareness, but haven't yet found an approach that ensures that all power differences are legitimate and based on merit. For continuous improvement in this area, we need to remain open to new approaches and be willing to experiment, even though it may be difficult.

Power Distance. How one uses power and influence is influenced by cultural norms and values. One important example is power distance, which was introduced along with other important cultural values in Concept 2. Power distance refers to how power is divided among people and how much perceived distance there is between people at different power levels.

"When in a high-power distance society, the relationship between bosses and subordinates is one of dependence. When in a low-power distance society, the relationship between bosses and subordinates is one of interdependence" (Rutledge, 2011). In a low-power distance culture, a leader might ask for a subordinate's opinion before making a decision. The subordinate will most likely feel comfortable giving an opinion, knowing that their ideas help the leader make a well-informed decision.

In a high-power distance culture, workers do not typically make suggestions to leaders because doing so would be seen as disrespectful and challenging. In fact, if asked for an opinion, the person would likely give the answer they think the leader wants to hear.

Understanding power distance can help you understand the people with whom you work. For example, you can understand the reluctance of a co-worker from a high-power distance culture to speak up in a meeting.

Also, be aware that your well-meaning behavior may cause discomfort to some people with whom you work. For example, often – with nothing but good intentions – some people may seek to share power when working in groups. But this can challenge other people. Say, for example, a college teacher wants her students to feel comfortable expressing their opinions, and she wants everyone to feel equal in the discussion. As part of this, she asks the class to call her by her first name. Many students would be happy to do this. However, some students, notably those from high-power distance cultures, may struggle with it. Their perception of power differences would not allow them to use a teacher's first name.

Power in Organizations. It would be nice to believe that power in organizations is earned through talent, experience, and time on the job. However, many of us recognize that such a belief may be wishful thinking, and is it is for this reason that this workbook was developed.

Not every person has earned the same level of power, and not everyone has the skills to manage power appropriately. Still, you must work to ensure that each individual – regardless of their culture or background – has access to opportunities for growth and to take on the power they have earned. Knowing that a person comes from a high-power distance culture is not a reason to deny them power; instead, use that knowledge and have open conversations aimed at helping them advance.

What to do:

☐ Make sure you are clear about the limits of your legitimate power--what you can and cannot ask of others simply because of your organizational position.

☐ Consider how power is distributed in your organization and in your team so that contrary opinions can be voiced without fear of negative consequences.

☐ When working with people, be considerate of how their behavior may be affected by their values around power distance.

Other actions:

☐ _____

☐ _____

☐ _____

☐ _____

☐ _____

☐ _____

Remember

✓ Everyone has some type of power.

✓ If you sense that some groups or individuals in your organization seem to lack power, prejudices or biases may be influencing who has the opportunity to advance and take control.

✓ A person from a low-power distance culture may readily provide input to people at higher levels in the organization, even if they are not asked.

✓ A person from a high-power distance culture may struggle to express opinions to higher-ups, even when asked. Encourage contrary opinions to be voiced without fear of negative consequences.

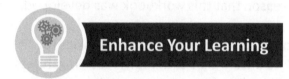

Enhance Your Learning

Managing cultural power differences is vital to understanding power in the workplace. It is also important to understand the systems of power in civic life including: physical force; wealth; state action (government); social norms; ideas; and numbers (people). Watch the following seven-minute video to understand the power dynamics in modern life:

How to Understand Power. Ted-Ed. (2014)		Available at: https://www.youtube.com/watch?v=c_Eutci7ack

Reinforce Your Learning

Bases of Power. For each of the seven bases of power, draw on your own experience and provide an example of how that particular power base has been used or abused.

1. Legitimate power.

_____

_____

2. Reward Power.

_____

_____

3. Coercive Power.

4. Expert Power.

5. Referent Power.

6. Information Power.

7. Connection Power.

What do you think is your strongest power base?

What is the power base you draw from most frequently?

What power base is valued most in your organization? For example, does your organization tend to place the highest value on people with expert technical skills? One way to analyze how power works in your organization is to consider the power bases associated with the most influential people in your organization

Navigate Unconscious Biases

Perceptions of power and power-differential is just one of the factors affecting how people in the work setting relate to each other. We also relate to others through a personal screen of assumptions, which can include positive and negative biases and prejudices. Too often, we do not realize we are biased or prejudiced, and you cannot fix a problem you do not know you have.

Negative bias against an individual or group can limit the potential of those who could, if treated without bias, make valuable contributions to the organization. Thus, it serves no useful purpose in the workplace. A productive, successful organization must embrace diversity and support an environment where people want to come to work. This means that each of us must be aware of our biases, know how they affect others, and commit to overcoming or, at least, not acting on, any negative biases.

"The flip side of diversity is discrimination" (Mahdawi, 2016). And discrimination is antithetical to productivity and profit. The good news is that unconscious bias is not permanent – it can be changed (Dasgupta, 2013, as cited in UCSF, n.d.).

Here is what you need to know about navigating unconscious biases:

A bias is a preference for, or against, a certain person, a group of people, or a thing. An unconscious bias is a bias that we are unaware of. It happens outside our control, automatically, as our lower brain makes quick judgments and assessments of people and situations. These judgments happen quickly and below full conscious awareness. They are triggered quickly and crudely, based on our stored emotional memories. Our background, cultural values, and life experiences shape these stored memories and thus our biases. We each have unconscious beliefs about various social, cultural and identity groups.

We filter much of what we do through our unconscious biases. For example, we may drive past a restaurant if some lights are out on their sign because we think it is of lower quality. Or we may feel a person is not intelligent or educated because of their accent or appearance. Or, we believe that someone is not likely to be a good leader because of their height or weight. Every day we make such unconscious assessments of people, things, and situations, and these assessments impact our behavior.

In the workplace, such unconscious perceptions and attitudes can negatively affect our ability to work with people who we perceive are different from us.

What can can you do about your unconscious biases?

Continuing our discussion, unconscious bias is our tendency to categorize or label someone else without being aware that we are doing it. We quickly decide that the person missing a front tooth is poor and uneducated. We consider the person who stutters or has an accent to be unintelligent. We may make other decisions about a man with a shaved head and body piercings, or someone with dark skin and a gold tooth or a woman wearing a hijab. We make assumptions without even thinking about them, and the assumptions guide our behavior.

- It can be challenging to overcome unconscious biases. One illustration that is commonly given to demonstrate this effort to do this, is telling someone: "Do not think of a pink elephant. Do not do it! Clear your mind and think of anything except an elephant, and certainly, do not think of a pink one holding a ball on its trunk." Most people will admit that far from not seeing a pink elephant, that is exactly what came into their mind's eye. Why? Because it is almost impossible to tell yourself not to think a certain way. By thinking it in the first place, you have thought of it.

- The fact is that instead of saying, "I'm not biased" or "I won't be biased," recognize when you are under the control of bias. Then call yourself out on that thinking and make an effort to think differently.

Become Aware of Your Unconscious Biases. The most important thing we can do to change our unconscious biases is to make the unconscious conscious. We must be aware of our biases and associated behavior before we can change them.

Following are some strategies you can use to help reduce or eliminate your unconscious biases (UCSF, n.d.):

- Being self-aware is an essential part of overcoming unconscious biases (see "What to Do" and "Reinforce Your Learning" below).

- Understanding the nature of bias is important. Biases grow out of our normal human need to put things into categories. This allows us to process things quickly and without too much scrutiny. To "unbundle" our beliefs about others we have to open up the category, and slow down the "automatic" processing by deep thinking and questioning.

- Talking to others – those similar and dissimilar to you – can be useful. Talking about your biases, and hearing about those that others have, can increase your awareness and provide insight into what you need to learn. Such conversations need to occur in a safe place, where everyone feels free to express their beliefs without ridicule.

- Participating in formal training to reduce bias in the workplace can be helpful.

At an organizational level, unconscious bias can be a factor in decisions about recruitment, hiring, promotions, contract negotiations, and salary discussions.

- Eliminating bias can be challenging. On a personal level, training like this and striving to check for bias in your decision-making process can help.

- Including diversity in a mission statement can be helpful, as can fostering a culture that values diversity.

- Sometimes, however, stronger actions may be required to ensure that hiring decisions are not biased. Such actions can include stripping names from resumes, conducting more phone interviews, and taking other steps to make it more difficult to detect differences that are not relevant to the job early in the selection process.

- Set objectives, goals, and indicators for hiring, evaluation, and promotion (UCSF, n.d.).

- Develop criteria or a performance assessment tool that is standard across the organization (UCSF, n.d.).

- Create a structured interview process for hiring (UCSF, n.d.).

- Train leaders in diversity and navigating unconscious bias and discrimination to focus on thinking through ways to minimize the effect of unconscious bias. Everyone has biases and if we aren't aware of these, we can't adjust our behaviors. A place to start may be identifying where bias can really affect operations (e.g. recruitment, promotions, contracts) and thinking through processes and systems that can minimize the impact of bias.

What to do:

☐ Examine your biases by doing an online search of "diverse faces."

☐ Look at the faces and take note of your emotional reactions to some of them.

☐ Reflect on your emotional reactions and what they may be telling you about your beliefs, unconscious biases, or fears. What might you need to change?

Other actions:

☐ _____

☐ _____

☐ _____

☐ _____

☐ _____

☐ _____

Remember

✓ Unconscious bias is just that, a bias you do not realize you have. Taking time to examine your behaviors in certain situations for evidence of bias will help you make the unconscious conscious. Checking your biases will increase your effectiveness in working in a diverse environment.

✓ Remember: "Biases come in all forms. There are biases against each generation, people with disabilities, LGBTQ people, working parents – even a person's height can cause bias! It's important to realize that all biases hurt the success of organizations. By creating an environment for open dialogue, you can make a strong effort to address this issue" (Loehr, 2016).

✓ An unconscious bias is not a permanent quality. It can be changed.

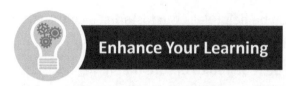

Implicit bias exists when people unconsciously hold attitudes toward others or associate stereotypes with them. Watch the following eight-minute video to learn more.

University of Texas - McCombs School of Business. *Implicit Bias | Concepts Unwrapped.* (2018).		Available at: https://www.youtube.com/watch?v=OoBvzI-YZf4

Take a Test and Learn about Yourself. Harvard University created an Implicit Association Test to help uncover unconscious bias.

Go to the following link and read about IAT and the test itself. Then, click "Take a Test" and choose one or more of the tests. They will help you better understand your biases.

Go to the Harvard Implicit Association Test website:

https://implicit.harvard.edu/implicit/education.html

Unconscious Bias. We all have some unconscious biases about some people in some situations. Recognizing this and thinking it through can go a long way toward ensuring that any underlying bias does not negatively affect your work relationships. Use these activities to uncover and reflect on your biases.

1. Sit back, relax, and close your eyes. Imagine meeting people who are different from you. Imagine that you walk up to a person whose skin color and accent are different from yours. You introduce yourself and shake hands. How do you feel about this person? Did you instantly make some type of judgment? Why? Where did that judgment come from?

2. Take a walk, preferably in a place where you know you will encounter diverse people, such as a restaurant or shopping mall. Notice each person and imagine greeting them. Think about who some of these people are and how they are different from you. Are you imaging positive interactions or negative ones? If negative, what can you do to picture positive ones?

As you do these activities, consider your reactions. Did your heart race when you imagined walking up to a particular type of person? Did you mentally roll your eyes when you looked at another person? Who made you feel anxious or fearful? Who made you feel more or less powerful?

Take some time to reflect on what you felt and how you processed those feelings. Keep these feelings and insights in mind through the rest of the course and think about what you can do to "navigate your unconscious biases."

Communicate and Enhance Respect Across Cultures

Our ability to communicate effectively is arguably one of the most important skill sets we have. We communicate almost all the time: when we hail a taxi, pay for groceries, go to a job interview, answer emails. Even the way we stand, smile, or wave are forms of communication. Each time we interact with another person, our every facial expression, gesture, and sound communicates something to that person.

Even when we make an extra effort to be clear and accurate in sharing our thoughts and feelings with others, we sometimes fail to do so. Messages get distorted, only partially heard, or misinterpreted. Miscommunication is common, even among people who know each other well. We miscommunicate with our families, friends, and people in the workplace. And, just as other people don't always receive our messages with accurate understanding, we don't always understand their messages to us. Sometimes, we don't know what they mean by the words they use, or we misread their facial expressions, or we don't truly listen.

If we so easily miscommunicate with people we know and with whom we share a culture, imagine how many misunderstandings can result when communicating with people we do not know well and who come from a different culture. Yet, we cannot do our jobs successfully, or develop productive work relationships, if we cannot communicate effectively.

Here is what you need to know about communication and respect across cultures:

Communication can be strongly influenced by unconscious bias. Once you are aware of your biases, one way to ensure that you do not act or communicate in a biased way is to visualize your interactions with people before you have them (Loehr, 2016):

- "Psychological research shows that visualizing a particular situation can create the same effects behaviorally and psychologically as actually experiencing the situation. In addition, brain studies reveal that mental imagery impacts several cognitive processes in the brain, including attention, perceptions, planning, and memory. This means you can train your brain for action through visualization."

- "What should you visualize? You can imagine yourself in a positive and productive meeting with team members who are different from you."

To work effectively with others, we must show respect, be open to ideas, and manage conflict. All of these require skills in communicating with others. Remember, communication is not just about what you **say** when speaking with your coworkers, it is also about what you express through your **body language** and **tone of voice,** and **how you communicate in writing**.

The way communications within your organization are handled is also important: the methods used, the type of information exchanged, the quantity and frequency of messages, and the channels or flow. Are messages predominantly top down, bottom up, lateral or a mixture? Are communications more formal or more informal? What is the organization's dominant protocol for communications between its members? Does that protocol show respect for people from different cultures?

Following the guidelines below can help you contribute to a respectful work climate:

- Be timely in all communications. For example, talking to someone about a problem is more effective if you do so near the time when the problem situation occurred.

- If a conversation becomes negative or if you become angry, do not say things you will regret. Instead, politely say you need some time and then walk away and think objectively about what happened. Take time to calm down. When you are ready, tell the other person you would like to continue the conversation. Taking a "time out" is also a good idea if the other person is showing anger or discomfort.

- Be understanding of people who do not communicate the same way you do. For example, people in some cultures may be reluctant to deliver bad news, while people in other cultures may be eager to report an issue so it can be dealt with quickly. Or, people in some cultures may be more animated and use more body language than you are accustomed to seeing.

- Although communication habits vary from individual to individual, it is important to keep cultural norms in mind when you communicate with someone whose background differs from yours. For example, some cultures are team-oriented while others are more focused on individuals. As a result, some people may be uncomfortable working alone, while others may need extra support, at least initially, to work effectively in a team.

- Do not fear conflict. Healthy conflict handled respectfully can lead to new ideas and innovations and stronger work relationships.

- Be aware that gestures and symbols may have different meanings in different cultures. Ask for clarity whenever you aren't sure you understand the meaning of a gesture, and be ready to explain what you mean by a gesture you use if the other person seems unclear. Always err on the side of caution and give people the benefit of the doubt.

- If you are unsure whether something is appropriate to do or say, do not do or say it.

- If you feel that someone has offended you in some way, take time to think about why they might have done what they did. Do not assume, without further consideration, that it was an intentional offense. Think about different things they might have meant to convey. Then, calmly and respectfully talk with the person to clarify their meaning.

- When you know you will be working with people from a particular culture, get some basic information about that culture. Do some research or speak with other people who have knowledge about the culture.

From employee handbooks to signs in the waiting room, from water cooler conversations to formal presentations to clients – how you communicate matters. Keeping differences among people in mind will enhance your effectiveness as a communicator.

What to do:

☐ Learn some basics about the culture of a co-worker whose cultural background is different from yours.

☐ Make a list of what to do and not to do when communicating with co-workers from different cultures.

☐ Commit to building your interpersonal communication skills: both speaking and listening.

Other actions:

☐ _____

☐ _____

☐ _____

☐ _____

☐ _____

Remember

✓ While culture affects a person's communication style, remember that people are also individuals. Every culture will have effective communicators and those who are not so effective, outgoing people and shy people, opinionated people and silent types, and so forth.

✓ It can be hard to communicate clearly with people who share our culture and background, so it is reasonable that communication will be even more challenging with people from other cultures and backgrounds.

✓ When communicating with people from different cultures, do:

  o Be clear in your language, enunciation, and voice.

  o Ask questions if you are unsure what the other person is saying, and listen.

  o Restate what you think the other person is saying for clarification.

  o Ask, politely, if the other person understands what you are saying.

  o Look for common ground.

✓ When communicating with people from different cultures, do not:

  o Use jargon or slang.

  o Raise your speaking volume: this comes across as anger.

  o Cast blame or lose your patience.

Watch the following five-minute video to learn more about communication and respect across cultures. Consider how you can apply this information in your work:

Cultural Diversity – Tips for Communicating with Cultural Diversity. Speak First. (2009)		Available at: https://www.youtube.com/watch?v=ZDvLk7e2Irc

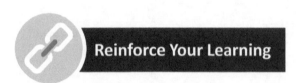

Effective Communication. List three things you can do in your workplace to help ensure effective communication among people of different backgrounds and cultures:

_____

_____

_____

_____

_____

_____

_____

_____

_____

_____

_____

_____

_____

_____

_____

Recognize Hot Buttons and Respond Appropriately to Conflict

They say you can tell a lot about a person by watching their behavior when things go wrong. How you handle conflict reveals a lot about who you are as a person. Sometimes, we deal with people who seem to thrive on conflict and drama, looking for ways to push other people's "hot buttons." Other times, those proverbial buttons get pushed by accident, for example, when we assume that another person shares our opinion on an issue, only to discover we are very far apart.

Regardless of how conflict begins, knowing how to manage it is crucial to working well with others.

Here is what you need to know about responding appropriately to conflict in the workplace:

Depending on the situation, it is sometimes best to avoid hot button topics. However, in other situations it may be best to discuss the topic. For example, with the "mask mandate" it may be better to "air it out" and explain why as an organization, we have chosen to move forward in the designated way.

You probably also have heard not to talk about politics, religion, and social issues at work unless the topic specifically relates to your work. However, how can you accommodate and be inclusive if you don't know certain aspects of these topics about someone? For example, if I don't know Mary is Muslim, then we wouldn't make the effort to keep food and drinks out of sight or not plan an office lunch during Ramadan when Muslims worldwide do not eat or drink anything from dawn until sunset.

If a hot button topic is work-related, separate opinions from people. For example, if your team is deciding whether to implement new software in a foreign country, avoid statements like, "You're crazy to think that" or "You couldn't be more wrong" when someone disagrees with your position. Stick to the relevant facts and avoid blaming or insulting someone else.

When you discuss controversial topics at work, either with people in your organization or with customers, or people from other organizations, keep these tips in mind:

- Focus on the ideas, not the people involved.

- Speak in facts, not generalizations, insults, or opinions.

- Focus on the job.

- Keep the interaction from becoming personal.

- Realize that conflict is positive when it is resolved in a way that leads to better decisions and improved work relationships.

- When necessary, agree to disagree. Sometimes it is wise for you and the other person or persons involved to take time out to reconsider your positions, gather more information, and return another time to continue seeking a resolution of benefit to the organization.

Reduce the incidence of non-work-related conflict:

- Avoid stereotypes.

- Use culturally appropriate terminology. If you don't know what is appropriate, ask someone who's knowledge and opinions you trust.

- Show respect for people whose backgrounds and experiences differ from yours.

- Demonstrate emotional intelligence, especially empathy or the ability to put yourself in another person's situation and understand how they feel.

- Demonstrate social intelligence, which is the ability to build productive relationships with others, especially with people whose backgrounds differ from yours.

Regardless of how cohesive a group may be, recognize that conflict will happen. Follow these tips when discord arises:

- Never raise your voice, even if you feel stressed. Take some deep breaths and if necessary, step away for a moment to regain composure.

- Simple misunderstandings can lead to more significant problems. If you have difficulty making your point, take some time to collect your thoughts and then rephrase your ideas. Ask the other person to tell you what they thought you said and then reclarify if necessary.

- Likewise, if you are confused about something someone said, repeat their statement back to them and if needed, ask for clarification. Restating what you heard can help you and the other person gain clarity, and asking questions will often lead to a more positive discussion.

In a group where you seem to be the lone dissenter, it may be necessary to take a break from the discussion and reevaluate your stance. Try these tips:

- Consider the points presented by the others and weigh them against your thoughts. Look for common ground.

- If you cannot reach an agreement, ask questions to understand more specifically where you disagree. You may find you agree on many issues, and perhaps disagree on only one or two. Work to resolve those differences. Or you might bring in an outside party to offer new ideas or a more productive approach.

- Never underestimate the power of a well thought out compromise. You may need to agree to disagree, at least in that discussion. On another day, you may be able to resolve the conflict.

If someone else in the discussion is the lone dissenter, do not immediately dismiss their input. Consider their ideas, and remember it almost always helps to ask questions.

Relationships can be damaged when people do not think before they speak. It is a simple mistake that can have devastating effects. When in doubt about whether to say something during a disagreement, remember to THINK. Ask yourself the following questions about what you are thinking about saying:

T	Is it true?
H	Is It helpful?
I	Is it inspiring?
N	Is it necessary?
K	Is it kind?

Additionally, remember it is not necessarily what you say but how you say it. As Winston Churchill said, "Tact is the ability to tell someone to go to hell in such a way that they look forward to the trip." Consider how your message will be received and choose words and actions that produce understanding and a positive reception.

When dealing with people with whom you often disagree, be aware of that and avoid both your and their trigger points. Here are some tips:

- Never say anything personal. For example, you may think the person is not logical, but calling out that "flaw" will cause more problems. Personal attacks never help.

- Find something to compliment, commend, or encourage the person. For instance, thanking them for refilling the copy paper, being on time, or producing a well-written report can set a positive tone. However, depending on the person, this could come across as condescending. Being respectful and starting on common ground is key.

Above all, keep in mind the "Golden Rule" or theory of reciprocity: People tend to react to you in the same way you treat them. You cannot expect to cultivate healthy working relationships in which you are respected unless you treat others respectfully.

Finally, understanding the place where you are doing business or providing service can help avoid potential problems. "For example, Pepsi lost its dominant market share to Coke in Southeast Asia when Pepsi changed the color of its vending machines to light 'Ice' [SIC] blue. The company failed to understand that light blue is associated with death and mourning in that region." (Lumen, n.d.).

What to do:	Other actions:
☐ Next time you are interacting, and it becomes hostile, use THINK to guide what you say.	☐ _____
	☐ _____
☐ Have a plan about how you will respectfully exit from a hostile interaction that seems to be growing out of control.	☐ _____
	☐ _____
☐ Develop a belief that conflicts can be resolved in healthy ways, with positive outcomes.	☐ _____

 **Remember**

✓ Avoid "hot button" issues in the workplace. Politics, religion, and other contentious topics are best left outside the workplace. However, if work-related, address by getting the facts and separating opinions from people.

✓ When handled well, differences of opinion can lead to new knowledge and innovations. Be open to hearing and understanding the ideas of others.

✓ Remember that your opinion is just that, your opinion. People with other experiences may think and feel differently and have different opinions.

✓ Do not fear conflict. Healthy conflict that is handled respectfully can lead to new ideas and innovations.

 Enhance Your Learning

Watch the following six-minute video to learn more about diversity and cultural differences at the workplace and how to get along with others by Leadership with Mike..

Managing diversity and cultural differences at workplace - how to get along with others. (2018)		Available at: https://www.youtube.com/watch?v=Kqixxo_yu4A

Fostering Diversity, Equity, and Inclusion in the Workplace

Reinforce Your Learning

Diffusing Negative Emotions. If you (or another person) start to get angry, impatient or frustrated during a conversation, what are three things you can do to keep the negative emotions from worsening?

"Everybody has a hot button. Who is pushing yours? While you probably cannot control that person, you CAN control the way you react to them."

— Source Unknown

Improve Workplace Relationships

"Companies lucky enough to have a workforce as diverse as the population find themselves armed with many perspectives, views and ideas that add strength to their ability to strategize, communicate and deliver" (Feigenbaum, 2018).

While most, if not all, organizations are growing in diversity, some organizations are not doing very well in fostering diversity and helping employees to work together effectively. As stated earlier, workforce diversity brings many benefits to an organization, but it also presents some challenges. Clashes will happen, relationships will be stressed at times, and some members of the workforce will prefer to "do things as we always have" rather than change behaviors and ways of thinking to embrace diversity.

Here is what you need to know about improving workplace relationships in a multi-cultural workforce:

Two important aspects for improving work relationships are ***cultural norms*** and ***effective communication***. Developing *cultural norms* or shared expectations help guide the behaviors of workgroups. Cultural norms are the standards that guide work groups, such as no smoking while working or no gossiping or making fun of people behind their backs. Effective communication employs both verbal and non-verbal communication methods to build interpersonal relationships, which at its core, requires people to get to know each other.

When you work in a team, realize that the team members will work together better when they have a shared mission or expectations, have developed their own ground rules, and have built trust with each other. To build trust, team members need time to learn about the backgrounds, skills, interests, work habits, ways of communicating, and aspirations of other members. This may take a bit more time with a diverse team than with a more homogeneous one. When a team is first formed, and when new members join an established team, it important to provide some opportunities for social interaction, even if only a few minutes of sharing treats during a break.

Be a role model. Strive to work on your behavior and demonstrate productive team behavior to others. It can make a difference. Be flexible and keep an open mind:

- When brainstorming with others, try to remember that we all have unique experiences from which we draw our values, beliefs and ideas.

- If someone presents what seems to be an unactionable idea or plan, do not automatically discount it. It may have merit or be a steppingstone toward a plausible solution, but you will not discover this if you do not listen.

When you are involved with a diverse group of people, understand that not everyone will work and communicate the same way, therefore it is beneficial to establish norms or ground rules for acceptable behavior and communication. This provides baselines from where to navigate. For instance, some people are not comfortable speaking face-to-face or via the phone and communicate more effectively through email. In this case, honor this preference by keeping phone calls to a minimum and focusing your attention on emails as the norm.

Recognizing group norms is also important when preparing for a meeting with a partner from outside of the organization and internal communications. Again, establishing group norms or providing standards during onboarding is beneficial for organizational work. Sometimes it may be necessary to over-communicate with new coworkers until a group norm is established or re-established. When communicating in-person, keep in mind that gestures and mannerisms can mean different things in different cultures.

- Take note of your coworkers' gestures, other non-verbal behaviors and how different they might when communicating face-to-face. Be respectful of boundaries or comfort zones. Bear in mind that a nuance such as avoiding prolonged eye-contact or refraining from handshaking may be a cultural norm rather than what you may consider to be bad manners. Also, do not assume that someone agrees with what you are saying just because they are smiling and nodding as you speak. They could simply be acknowledging that you are speaking.

Attempt to know your coworkers as individuals. Learn about their life experiences and how those have shaped them and their thought process, as this can help you gain valuable insight as to their talents and temperament. This insight can also strengthen your work relationships, as well as help your coworkers make the most of their talents and abilities.

Coworkers often gather outside the workplace to socialize. Doing so builds comradery and strengthens interpersonal relationships, but it can also lead to feelings of isolation and resentment among associates who do not participate in these functions. Make an extra effort to invite and include everyone on your team when planning social outings. If you know someone has an issue with large crowds, invite them to a smaller gathering or spend a coffee break making small talk with them. These simple things can make a tremendous difference in team morale, productivity, and can be beneficial in developing and understanding group norms.

In his classic, long-time best-selling book *How to Win Friends and Influence People*, Dale Carnegie gave sound advice about working well with others: You must legitimately find something about the person to like or they will see you as a phony. When you work with someone with whom you are uncomfortable or do not care for, try to find some common ground so you can honestly share something constructive. (Carnegie, 1936). Whether it is their kids, a hobby, the shirt they are wearing – find any legitimate, honest thing to be positive about, and it will give you a foundation to build on.

What to do:

☐ When working with someone from a different cultural group, pay attention to how their gestures and non-verbal behaviors differ from yours.

☐ Allow teams comprised of members from diverse backgrounds ample time for the members to develop trust.

☐ Influence the behavior of others by showing your commitment to diversity, inclusion and teamwork.

Other actions:

☐ _____

☐ _____

☐ _____

☐ _____

☐ _____

Remember

✓ Two important aspects for improving work relationships are cultural norms and effective communication.

✓ Cultural norms are the standards that guide work groups, such as no smoking while working or no gossiping or making fun of people behind their backs.

✓ Effective communication employs both verbal and non-verbal communication methods to build interpersonal relationships, which at its core, requires people to get to know each other.

✓ To work well with others: You must legitimately find something about the person to like or they will see you as a phony.

Enhance Your Learning

Watch the following three-minute video to learn some simple ways to build relationships. Consider how you can apply this information in your work:

How to Build Trust and Relationships. Litmos Heroes. (2014)		Available at: https://www.youtube.com/watch?v=wtNOq1Bwtt4

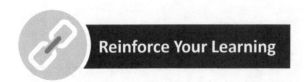

Reinforce Your Learning

Be a Role Model. What does your behavior reveal to coworkers about your attitudes and beliefs regarding diversity and inclusion? What are you saying and doing that demonstrates your openness to building productive relationships with all coworkers? List things you are doing that support a positive value for diversity and inclusion, and things you are doing that might undermine that value. Use these to guide you in becoming the best diversity role model you can be.

Things that support:

_____

_____

_____

_____

_____

_____

Things that undermine:

_____

_____

_____

_____

_____

_____

Cultivate an Inclusive Culture

In order to develop an inclusive culture, an organization can create posters, mission statements, team outings, and even design spirit t-shirts, but what really matters when establishing an inclusive culture is action. If diversity becomes a real part of an organization's culture, it is followed with action in recruiting, onboarding, training, coaching, mentoring, and assessing – throughout the employment life cycle.

Walmart learned the hard way that attracting customers requires actions based on understanding the importance of cultural differences. They discovered that diversity is about more than just opening a store in a different cultural location. When Walmart opened its first store in Mexico --

> "It modeled the Wal-Mart [sic] stores in Mexico after its stores in the United States, with a stand-alone store surrounded by large parking lots. But it soon realized this was a problem. Many of the customers rode on buses to the store. This meant customers had to walk through the parking lot to get to the store and could only buy what they could carry back to the bus. To address this, Wal-Mart added shuttle buses that took customers to and from the store." (Lumen, n.d.).

Walmart had the right idea in trying to reach new customers, but they did not understand the cultural differences in Mexico that would affect how customers shopped. When you work with diverse populations, you run the risk of being less successful if you do not understand such differences. To start, commit to building a culture in your organization that values diversity.

Here is what you need to know about cultivating an inclusive culture:

While a growing number of organizations have embraced a goal of developing an inclusive culture, it is not necessarily easy. We must recognize that good relationships take time and effort. An inclusive culture must be intentionally developed, and a large part of this development is recognizing that some practices that have traditionally been accepted, without question, as "universal" norms need to be challenged. As these practices begin to be analyzed and changed, the organization's culture will also change; ideally, to a culture where every member feels included and valued.

If they are to create and maintain a respectful, all-inclusive climate, the organization's leaders must be dedicated, continuous learners. And, the best way to learn about a different culture or group is through someone with an intimate, first-hand knowledge of that culture or group. This is the same principle as asking a local person for ideas on what to see and do when traveling through their area. In short, if a leader in the organization needs to find out more about the cultural norms in Paris, France, they should seek out a Parisian.

In Paris, for example, it is considered rude not to address a worker in a store or restaurant without first saying hello or bonjour.

It is impossible to know every nuance of every culture, but when you take the time to gain understanding about a specific culture's traditions or taboos, you can share what you have learned with others in the organization, thus expanding understanding.

- For example, you will never see a Disney employee pointing with their index finger alone, as it is considered rude in many cultures.

- Holding a thumb up is positive in the U.S., but negative in some cultures.

Attempting to gain understanding of people of other cultures means not only learning about their cultures, but also being open to criticism when you have unintentionally crossed the lines of what is considered acceptable to that culture.

- When someone from a culture different than yours tells you that a particular word, gesture, or phrase is unacceptable to them, tell the person you appreciate learning this and take immediate action to modify your behavior.

- You can then pass on your knowledge respectfully when you encounter another someone else unwittingly exhibiting that culturally inacceptable act.

- People often do not realize the harm in perpetuating certain words or behaviors that are offensive to others. It may help to consider a behavior that annoys you if you stop and consider whether or not that behavior might be related to culture. For example, if someone is late for a meeting, rather than becoming annoyed or offended you might find that "time" is more flexible in that person's culture. In the same way, you may speak or act as you usually do, and not realize that your habits may annoy or offend others. It is to your benefit to become aware of those habits, and work to adjust them.

Sometimes we find knowledge and inspiration in the most unlikely places. The animated movie *Barnyard* provides the following nugget of wisdom: "A strong man stands up for himself, a stronger man stands up for others." This is a particularly useful idea when cultivating relationships with people of differing backgrounds, especially those who are part of a minority group in your organization.

- Do not be afraid to speak up on behalf of someone else. Do not speak for them but rather speak to any offense against them that you have observed. Address the offending party respectfully.

- Do not assume that someone else will speak up; be the proactive person in such situations.

Encourage others to also speak out when they notice cultural insensitivity or inappropriateness. There is strength in numbers. As more people consistently address such problems, the more likely your organization will be to experience positive change.

Ensure that your culture of diversity is embraced in recruiting, onboarding, training, coaching, mentoring and assessing performance throughout the employment life cycle.

What to do:

☐ Do not ignore inappropriate or culturally insensitive behavior.

☐ If you are offended by someone, respectfully explain the offense and accept any apology with grace.

☐ If you accidentally or unknowingly offend someone, offer an apology immediately. Be careful not to repeat the offending behavior.

Other actions:

☐ _____

☐ _____

☐ _____

☐ _____

☐ _____

 Remember

✓ Ignoring rude or inappropriate behavior makes you culpable. If you see a person being culturally insensitive or disrespectful of a person's "otherness," stand up for for the person being demeaned. As Gandhi said: "Be the change that you want to see in the world."

✓ If diversity becomes a real part of an organization's culture, it is followed by actions in recruiting, onboarding, training, coaching, mentoring, and assessing – throughout the employment life cycle.

 Enhance Your Learning

Watch the following two-minute video to learn a bit about unconscious bias and how you can help cultivate inclusion. Note that this video mentions the company whose HR staff created the video, but all concepts will likely apply to your organization.

Inclusion begins with you. EY Global. (2015).		Available at: https://www.youtube.com/watch?v=StKnycqjlUo

Review the following bog article and evaluate what ideas you might implement in your organization.

50+ Ideas for Cultivating Diversity and Inclusion at Your Company. LinkedIn Talent Blog. (2021).		Available at: https://www.linkedin.com/business/talent/blog/talent-acquisition/ideas-for-cultivating-diversity-and-inclusion

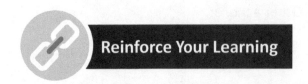

Reinforce Your Learning

Inclusive culture. Consider the area in which you work, or for which you are responsible. Whether you are hiring, training, or working with customers – whatever your job is – consider how you can influence the culture in that area to help everyone commit to inclusion. Brainstorm a few ideas below.

Implement Best Practices

We have discussed how diversity is a business necessity in today's marketplace, not just a warm and fuzzy idea. In Concept 1, we covered studies showing higher profits for organizations that foster diversity, and in Concept 6, we described how Pepsi lost market share by not understanding how color of equipment may affect buying choices in some cultures.

We also discussed that diversity must be part of an organization's culture and that embracing, and valuing diversity must come from the top. Simply using the right words – like diversity and inclusion – is not enough. The members of the organization must genuinely commit to behaviors that match the stated ideals.

We are what we do.

A commitment to diversity and inclusion means implementing and promoting best practices in support of these values, at the individual, group and organizational levels.

Here is what you need to know about best practices in diversity and inclusion, organizational culture, networking, and systematic reviews of processes and systems (e.g., recruitment, hiring, promotions):

- While an organization's culture is developed both top-down and bottom-up, effective diversity initiatives must be championed by top leadership and should be included in an organization's mission, vision, and values statements.

- Successful organizations address their goals of diversity and inclusion in various organizational statements for everyone to see, and link these to strategic planning initiatives.

- **Employment Advertising.** In recruiting and hiring, one best practice is to advertise jobs in areas and media where diverse audiences are reached. For example, hold career fairs at local colleges and trade schools which have a diverse student population.

- **Training.** Diversity training can be effective at all levels of an organization, but be aware that some concepts, and the ways they are presented, can upset some employees. To get the best benefit with the least upset, hire an experienced organization to conduct the training, one with an excellent track record and good referrals. Employees at all levels of the organization, including the highest leadership, should attend.

- Keep in mind that diversity training is generally not a "once and done" thing. You do not "finish" learning when the class ends. Diversity training is the start of something, the beginning of organization-wide behavioral change.

Affirmative Action. Laws and organizational policies enacted in the 1960's required specific quotas and programs to encourage educational and employment opportunities for women and other minorities. While affirmative action policies and programs were intended to have a positive impact on participation rates by previously underrepresented groups, the results were mixed.

- Many people felt it was a form of reverse discrimination against white males.

- Many states no longer have affirmative action laws.

- Many people today still believe it is positive and can help balance opportunity among groups.

Set Hiring Goals. Despite the ongoing debate about affirmative action, many organizations find it practical to set hiring goals using some type of affirmative action guidelines.

For example, it can be beneficial for an organization to set goals that will help align its workforce with the customers they serve or the places they do business. Recall, in our example from Concept 8, Walmart experienced problems with a new store in Mexico because they did not consider local shopping habits. Having project teams with customer-specific experience will help avoid such mistakes.

Keep in mind that this is not about checking a box and "saying" the organization has diversity. It is about strengthening the workforce by including new points of view and experiences.

Diversity Champions. Create champions. Engage specific knowledgeable individuals to champion diversity in your organization or workgroup. Encourage them to role model, start discussions, and work to generate enthusiasm for diversity initiatives.

Keep in mind that inclusion does not mean helping people who are different to behave the same as the dominant culture or group. Rather, it is about inviting everyone to share their unique viewpoints, perceptions and knowledge, and celebrating the strengths and gifts everyone brings to the organization.

Help people in your organization feel they belong. Employees who feel they belong are more likely to bring their best selves to work and to use their creativity and skills for the betterment of their fellow employees and the organization. It is unrealistic to expect employees to be highly engaged if they do not feel included.

Empathy. Empathy is important. If you can "put yourself in the other person's shoes," as they say, it is easier for you to understand them, appreciate their contributions, and interact with them in positive and respectful ways.

What to do:	**Other actions:**
☐ Be a champion of diversity in your workgroup.	☐ _____
	☐ _____
☐ Learn more about what other organizations are doing to create best practices that support a culture of diversity and inclusion.	☐ _____
	☐ _____
☐ Help individuals in your organization feel they belong and create opportunities for them to engage.	☐ _____
	☐ _____

 **Remember**

✓ Encourage a diverse culture and role model positive behavior.

✓ Diverse workplaces are more creative and productive.

✓ Changing an organization's culture takes time, but what you do each and every day can make the process faster and smoother. Every positive action you take moves your organization closer to having an inclusive culture and climate.

 **Enhance Your Learning**

Watch the following twenty-three-minute video to learn more about effective diversity practices. Consider how you can apply this information in your work:

Diversity, Equity & Inclusion | Workplace DEI Best Practices | OPERATOR INSIGHTS. (2021)		Available at: https://www.youtube.com/watch?v=AjLEHY04t4M

Check out these links to learn more about best practices and which organizations excel:

Forbes list of best workplaces for diversity:
https://www.forbes.com/sites/vickyvalet/2019/01/15/americas-best-employers-for-diversity-2019/#5598888e2bda

The Human Rights Campaign (HRC) diversity index:
https://www.hrc.org/campaigns/corporate-equality-index

The diversity best practices inclusion index:
https://www.workingmother.com/diversity-best-practices-inclusion-index-2018

Fortune Magazine's list of the 100 best workplaces places for diversity:
https://fortune.com/best-workplaces-for-diversity/

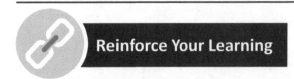

Reinforce Your Learning

Best Practices. Use the **Best Practices** inventory to identify what you know about your organization or workgroup's diversity and inclusion practices and to consider areas for improvement. Read the best practices below, and check or circle each one that you could apply or implement within your organization or workgroup.

BEST PRACTICES
_____ 1. Communicates diversity and inclusion as a critical component of an organization's strategic plan through regular communication channels.
_____ 2. Establishes clear non-discrimination policies and procedures across all workgroups and levels.
_____ 3. Establishes diversity processes that require adoption and implementation of essential literacies, anti-discrimination polices, inclusivity, and mental health and well-being programs.
_____ 4. Fosters diversity and inclusion as part of an organization's culture by incorporating them in recruiting, onboarding, training, coaching, mentoring, and assessment – throughout the employment life cycle.
_____ 5. Provides training for fostering a diverse and inclusive workplace and builds cross-cultural competence.
_____ 6. Helps individuals in an organization feel they belong by creating opportunities and interest groups for engagement within and outside of the workplace.
_____ 7. Facilitates sessions to help employees and leaders become aware of their behaviors and biases.
_____ 8. Manages unconscious bias by enlisting the support of peers and mentors.
_____ 9. Benchmarks best practices with other organizations or workgroups in recruitment, retention, and advancement of people from under-represented groups.
_____ 10. Integrates diversity of thought into decisions that affect talent acquisition, promotions, succession planning, and leadership development.
_____ 11 Creates a pipeline for more diverse talent by developing relationships with under-represented groups and organizations by assigning dedicated liaisons to each.
_____ 12. Takes steps to ensure greater equity for employees and their families in the form of comprehensive policies, benefits, and practices.
_____ 13. Provides diversity and inclusion resources that empower and support individuals to speak-up and share thoughts and ideas.
_____ 14. Includes diversity and inclusion outcomes in the goals or performance expectations of organizational leaders.
_____ 15. Measures diversity and inclusion related activities and their strategic impact and reports results and accomplishments on an ongoing basis.

Value Yourself

Throughout this course, we have discussed cultural, generational, and other differences that exist in today's workforce and the benefits available to organizations who embrace these differences. Diversity is about bringing a variety of experiences, knowledge, points of view, and talents to support an organization's mission. It is about everyone pulling together to do what is best for the organization, its stakeholders and customers, and society in general.

In Concept 4, we discussed unconscious bias and how bringing such biases to conscious awareness will help us truly see, and appreciate other people as individuals. In addition, before you can fully appreciate other people, you must understand and value yourself. Yes, we know, this sounds like "psychobabble" – you cannot love someone else until you love yourself. But it is true.

Prejudice, bigotry and discrimination come from ignorance and fear. To be accepting of others, you must begin from a place of confidence in who you are and a belief in your value. This will help you realize the intrinsic value of others, and how they can contribute to stronger relationships, more productive teams, and an organization that thrives in today's fast-paced, competitive and increasingly global market place.

When you value yourself, you just may find it easier to appreciate people who seem different from you because you will see your shared humanity.

Here is what you need to know about valuing yourself:

Legions of self-help books, videos, and podcasts are available to help people boost their self-esteem. Why? Because you need to believe in yourself to live your best life.

What is your best life? It does not mean you must own a mansion or sail a yacht. Your best life is about being the best you can be for yourself, your family, your organization, and society in general.

Recognize Your Strengths and Work to Improve Yourself. Being your best means taking stock of your attributes and behaviors on a regular basis. And, don't focus just on what you need to do better. Recognize what is amazing and awesome about you and give yourself credit for those things. Even things that may seem small and natural to you. Are you timely in keeping others informed? Great! Do you have patience with others? Excellent! Whatever your strengths, celebrate them.

Also consider what you could improve about yourself, the areas of opportunity if you will. No one is perfect. Without a doubt, you could do some things better. Recognize them, then create an improvement plan. The Japanese have a saying in business: kaizen. It means "continuous improvement." It is a goal that every organization and individual can strive toward: Always get better. And remember, "getting better" does not mean the same thing in all cultures!

Bring Your Whole Self to Work. This is important! Both to help others understand you and model how others can share their stories so you can understand them.

Okay, what does **bring your whole self to work** mean?

It highlights the idea that you will be less happy in your personal life and less effective in your work life if only part of you is in each place.

Bringing your whole self to work means being open and a bit vulnerable. You let other people get to know you, and that you take time to get to know them. It means you do not work somewhere where you have to hide your true self. You live authentically and feel safe and valued.

People who bring their whole selves to work are more engaged and more productive. They take fewer sick days and are happier.

What are some ways for you to bring your whole self to work? Do not be afraid to ask and answer questions or make mistakes. Open up, at least a bit, and get to know people while letting them get to know you. Look for opportunities to communicate with the people around you. Share. Be authentic, but also humble and empathetic. Be a whole person, not just a worker.

Take Care of Yourself. You must care for yourself, physically and emotionally. For example, good leaders know that before they can guide others, they must take care of themselves. No one can pay attention to other things when they are hungry, cold, or sick.

Exercise (just a 20 minute walk a few times a week counts!), eat healthful food (or even a little healthier), drink plenty of water, and get enough sleep (for most people at least seven hours a night). When you take care of your body, your body is more likely to function as you need it to function to ensure your productivity.

Emotional health also matters; it affects your physical health and ability to concentrate on the job at hand. Learn to manage your stress and emotions. If you have trouble in this area, do some research on your own, or talk to a professional about what concerns you.

Here are helpful activities to build into your life:

- Exercise

- Meditation

- More sleep

- Interests you enjoy

- Stress management and, when needed, give yourself a break from stress

- Sharing your feelings

Embrace a Growth Mindset. You may have noticed that you can often divide the people with whom you work into two types: those with fixed mindsets and those with growth mindsets. You want to be the latter.

A fixed mindset is when you believe that what you are now is all you can or will be. You are as smart, healthy, and happy now as you will ever be. This is it. And this mindset is not accurate.

A growth mindset is when you know you have the power to grow and change, and that changing yourself can change your circumstances. This is reality. You can always learn a new skill, gain knowledge, modify your behavior, and challenge yourself to do more. Know that and work on it.

What to do:	Other actions:
☐ Take the time to reflect on your sense of self-worth.	☐ _____
	☐ _____
☐ Work on your confidence and sense of self by reading about these topics.	☐ _____
☐ Think about your mindset: do you need to develop more growth-oriented beliefs?	☐ _____
	☐ _____

 **Remember**

✓ You must accept and believe in yourself before you can accept and believe in others.

✓ Writing positive statements can help.

     o For example, you might write, "I am a hard-working, ethical, and caring individual who values the work of others and gets the job done."

     o Write affirmations for yourself to highlight what you strive to be. As you recite your affirmations each day, internalize them and work to make them real.

Enhance Your Learning

Watch the following twelve-minute video to learn more about valuing yourself. Consider how you can apply this information in your work:

Bring Your Whole Self to Work. TEDx Talks. (2015)		Available at: https://www.youtube.com/watch?v=bd2WKQWG_Dg

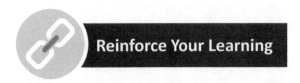

Reinforce Your Learning

Understand and Accept Yourself. Understanding and accepting other people requires that you first understand and value yourself. Write three things that you do that make you like and accept yourself, and three things you want to do or change to be even better:

Three things I do now that make me like and accept myself:

_____

_____

_____

_____

_____

Three things I want to do or change to make me even better:

_____

_____

_____

_____

_____

Summary

Diversity breeds creativity and innovation!

A diverse organization that effectively manages its diversity is a healthy organization. Diversity brings new ideas, new points of view, and new ways of thinking. It helps organizations meet the challenges they face today. To realize these benefits, organizational leaders must build cultures that are inclusive. Employees and leaders must understand the value inherent in diversity and be willing to work past differences to achieve the benefits it offers.

Consider what actions you can take to better understand and manage a diverse workplace, and to put your understanding of diversity into action. Consider how doing so will impact your work, asking yourself:

- Do I understand the value of diversity in the workplace?

- How does my personal behavior affect others in my workplace?

- What can I do every day to demonstrate my commitment to diversity?

- What should I do if I have questions about diversity issues in my workplace?

- Am I prepared to handle any challenging multicultural situations that may arise?

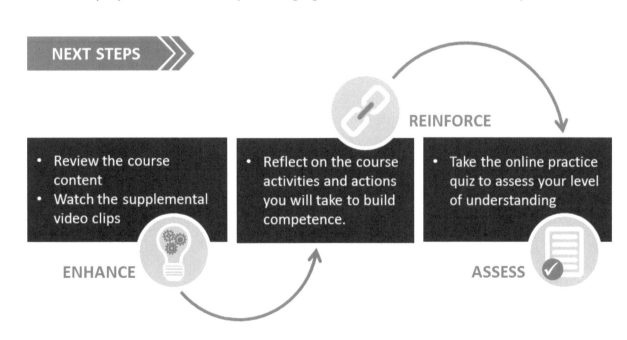

NEXT STEPS

REINFORCE

- Review the course content
- Watch the supplemental video clips

- Reflect on the course activities and actions you will take to build competence.

- Take the online practice quiz to assess your level of understanding

ENHANCE

ASSESS

Notes:

Fostering Diversity and Inclusion in the Workplace - Recap Checklist

Everyone in an organization must foster diversity and inclusion to benefit from the different points of view, knowledge, and experience that a diverse workforce offers.

1. Understand Diversity and Inclusion in the Workplace
- ❑ Recognize the value of diversity, equity, and inclusion in your workplace.
- ❑ Consider how having diverse leadership and a diverse workforce can benefit your organization.
- ❑ Understand that diversity is more than a buzzword. Diversity is good business.

2. Be Aware of Culture in Work Relationships
- ❑ Pay attention to people around you and be aware of differences and similarities.
- ❑ Recognize how you are different and be mindful of your behavior.
- ❑ Make an effort to understand and value the people with whom you work.

3. Consider Differences in Power and Influence
- ☐ Make sure you're clear about the limits of your legitimate power--what you can and cannot ask of others simply because of your organizational position.
- ☐ Consider how power is distributed in your organization and in your team so that contrary opinions can be voiced without fear of negative consequences.
- ☐ When working with people, be considerate of how their behavior may be affected by their values around power distance.

4. Navigate Unconscious Biases
- ☐ Examine your biases by doing an online search on "diverse faces."
- ☐ Look at the faces and take note of your emotional reactions to some of them.
- ☐ Reflect on your emotional reactions and what they may be telling you about your beliefs, unconscious biases, or fears. What might you need to change?

5. Communicate and Enhance Respect across Cultures
- ☐ Learn some basics about the culture of a co-worker whose cultural background is different from yours.
- ☐ Make a list of what to do and not to do when communicating with co-workers from different cultures.
- ☐ Commit to building your interpersonal communication skills: both speaking and listening.

6. Recognize Hot Buttons and Respond Appropriately to Conflict
- ☐ Next time you are interacting and it becomes hostile, use THINK to guide what you say.
- ☐ Have a plan about how you will respectfully exit from a hostile interaction that seems to be growing out of control.
- ☐ Develop a belief that conflicts can be resolved in healthy ways, with positive outcomes.

7. Improve Workplace Relationships
- ☐ When working with someone from a different cultural group, pay attention to how their gestures and non-verbal behaviors differ from yours.
- ☐ Allow teams comprised of members from diverse backgrounds ample time for the members to develop trust.
- ☐ Influence the behavior of others by showing your commitment to diversity, inclusion and teamwork.

8. Cultivate an Inclusive Culture
- ☐ Do not ignore inappropriate behavior.
- ☐ If you are offended by someone, explain the situation, and accept any apology with grace.
- ☐ If you accidentally offend someone, offer an apology immediately. Be careful not to repeat the behavior.

9. Implement Best Practices
- ☐ Be a champion of diversity in your workgroup.
- ☐ Learn more about what other organizations are doing to create best practices that support a culture of diversity and inclusion.
- ☐ Help individuals in your organization feel they belong and create opportunities for them to engage.

10. Value Yourself
- ☐ Take the time to reflect on your sense of self-worth.
- ☐ Work on your confidence and sense of self by reading about these topics.
- ☐ Think about your mindset: do you need to develop more growth-oriented beliefs?

Action Planning | **Competency #1** >> **Interpersonal Skills**
- appropriately Sociable; interacts Effectively with others

Briefly Describe how improvement in this competency will help you achieve important results or better meet your job responsibilities.

_____

_____

_____

_____

_____

_____

_____

List courses, books, and independent study opportunities that could help you develop this competency.

_____

_____

_____

_____

_____

_____

_____

_____

Identify one or more people who could help you, either as a role model or source of information. Write any questions you want to ask each person

What specific steps will you take?   **Start Date**   **Finished**

Action Planning **Competency #2** 〉〉

Interpersonal Relationship Building
- considers and responds appropriately to needs, feelings, and capabilities of others; seeks feedback and accurately assesses impact on others; provides helpful feedback; builds trust with others

Briefly Describe how improvement in this competency will help you achieve important results or better meet your job responsibilities.

_____

_____

_____

_____

_____

_____

_____

_____

List courses, books, and independent study opportunities that could help you develop this competency.

_____

_____

_____

_____

_____

_____

_____

_____

_____

Identify one or more people who could help you, either as a role model or source of information. Write any questions you want to ask each person

What specific steps will you take?	Start Date	Finished

Action Planning | **Competency #3** >>

Diverse Workforce
– recognizes the value of culture, ethnic, gender, and other differences; provides employment and development Opportunities for a diverse workforce

Briefly Describe how improvement in this competency will help you achieve important results or better meet your job responsibilities.

List courses, books, and independent study opportunities that could help you develop this competency.

Identify one or more people who could help you, either as a role model or source of information. Write any questions you want to ask each person

What specific steps will you take?	Start Date	Finished

The great courageous act that we must all do, is to have the courage to step out of our history and past so that we can live our dreams.

- Oprah Winfrey

Appendices

Part A. Knowledge Review Test – Answer Sheet

Part B. Knowledge Review Test - Questions

Part A. Knowledge Review Test – Answer Sheet

Because It is not always convenient to take on-line courses, we now offer the option for you to earn Professional Development Units (PDHs) through a process like a correspondence course. You can study the content of this workbook at home or work, complete the following knowledge review test, and then fax, mail, or email the answer sheet along with the payment fee noted on our website. You can also copy and paste your answers below into our website Contact Form to submit them. We will then email your certificate of completion to you, or if you prefer, we can mail it.

Alternatively, you can register for courses at www.centrestar.com and work through the material online, take the test, and download your certificate.

Course: **Fostering Diversity and Inclusion in the Workplace** (CPE 2214)

Name:

Email:

Address:

I certify that I have completed this test myself.   ____ Yes   ____ No

Signature: _____   Date: _____

Circle or check the best answer to each question.

1.	___ A	___ B	___ C	___ D	___ E
2.	___ A	___ B	___ C	___ D	___ E
3.	___ A	___ B	___ C	___ D	___ E
4.	___ A	___ B	___ C	___ D	___ E
5.	___ A	___ B	___ C	___ D	___ E
6.	___ A	___ B	___ C	___ D	___ E
7.	___ A	___ B	___ C	___ D	___ E
8.	___ A	___ B	___ C	___ D	___ E
9.	___ A	___ B	___ C	___ D	___ E
10.	___ A	___ B	___ C	___ D	___ E
11.	___ A	___ B	___ C	___ D	___ E
12.	___ A	___ B	___ C	___ D	___ E
13.	___ A	___ B	___ C	___ D	___ E
14.	___ A	___ B	___ C	___ D	___ E
15.	___ A	___ B	___ C	___ D	___ E
16.	___ A	___ B	___ C	___ D	___ E
17.	___ A	___ B	___ C	___ D	___ E
18.	___ A	___ B	___ C	___ D	___ E
19.	___ A	___ B	___ C	___ D	___ E
20.	___ A	___ B	___ C	___ D	___ E

Part B. Knowledge Review Test - Questions

CPE 2214 Fostering Diversity and Inclusion in the Workplace

1. Which of the following is true about diversity?
   A. It is nothing but a buzzword.
   B. It can only be achieved through affirmative action.
   C. Studies show diverse organizations have higher earnings.
   D. None of the above are true.

2. Diversity relates to differences in what?
   A. Skin color
   B. Language
   C. Age
   D. Gender
   E. All of the above

3. One study found that diverse juries performed better than juries made up of all white people.
   A. True
   B. False

4. When it comes to the workplace, which of the following is NOT true:
   A. We should not learn about different cultures because that is stereotyping.
   B. Diversity improves innovation.
   C. Cultural protocols refer to the customers, actions, codes, ethics, and behaviors that guide people of a particular culture or group
   D. All of the above are true.

5. Most Americans do not have any cultural protocols.
   A. True
   B. False

6. What is power distance?
   A. How much power a person has.
   B. How much power a person wants.
   C. The perceived distance between people of different power levels.
   D. How far a person is willing to go to take power from another person.

7. If a low-level worker in China is afraid to give his supervisor his opinion, this is an example of what?
   A. Poor self-esteem.
   B. High power distance.
   C. Low power distance.
   D. All of the above.

8. Unconscious bias cannot be changed.

    A.   True

    B.   False

9. Unconscious bias is what?

    A.   When a person is a racist and marches in Washington.

    B.   When a person hates people of other religions or is atheist.

    C.   When a person has a preference for, or against, a certain type of person or thing, even though they do not consciously realize it.

    D.   None of the above.

10. Communications refers to what?

    A.   Writing

    B.   Speaking

    C.   Body language

    D.   All of the above

11. Which of the following is NOT a good tip for communicating with diverse groups?

    A.   Be timely.

    B.   Use clear language.

    C.   Avoid jargon.

    D.   All of the above are good tips

12. Conflict should be avoided at all costs.

    A.   True

    B.   False

13. Which of the following are good things to say when communicating with diverse people?

    A.   Talk about politics.

    B.   Use phrases like "you are crazy".

    C.   Talk about social issues and religion.

    D.   None of the above are good choices.

14. In the acronym THINK what does the "I" stand for?

    A.   Incipient

    B.   Incredulous

    C.   Inspiring

    D.   Interesting

15. When working with a diverse group of people you should try to adapt your communication techniques to best accommodate your coworkers.

    A.   True

    B.   False

16. Which of the following is the most important part of diversity?

    A. Creating mission statements.

    B. Using the word "diversity" on posters.

    C. Creating diversity web pages.

    D. None of the above.

    E. All of the above are equally important.

17. Diversity should be implemented in which of the following?

    A. Recruitment.

    B. Orientation.

    C. Training.

    D. Coaching.

    E. All of the above.

18. What do we call the legal idea begun in the 1960s where laws and organizational policies specifically required certain quotas or policies to encourage more education and hiring of women and minorities?

    A. Affirmative action

    B. Affirmations in human resources

    C. Illegal

    D. None of the above

    E. All of the above

19. Bigotry and discrimination come from where?

    A. Hate

    B. Fear

    C. Religion

    D. Politics

20. Understanding and valuing yourself is an important part of accepting diversity in others.

    A. True

    B. False

Sources / Citations

Apple. (2017). *Apple – Inclusion & Diversity – Open*. Retrieved from,
https://www.youtube.com/watch?v=cvb49-Csq1o

Carnegie, D. (1936). *How to Win Friends and Influence People.* NY: Simon & Schuster.

Dixon, E., (2016). *Best Practices for Valuing Diversity*. Retrieved from,
https://www.youtube.com/watch?v=avMQQpjc-L0

EY Global. (2015). *Inclusion begins with you*. Retrieved from,
https://www.youtube.com/watch?v=StKnycqjlUo

Feigenbaum, E. (2018). *The Value of Diversity in the Workplace*. Small Business Chronicle.
Retrieved from, https://smallbusiness.chron.com/value-diversity-workplace-3035.html

French, J. and Raven, B. (1959). *The Bases of Social Power. In Studies in Social Power*, D.
Cartwright, Ed., pp. 150-167. Ann Arbor, MI: Institute for Social Research.

Harvard University. (2011). *Implicit Association Test (IAT).* Retrieved from,
https://implicit.harvard.edu/implicit/education.html

Include-Empower (2015). *Nine Cultural Power Differences You Need to Know*. Retrieved from,
https://cultureplusconsulting.com/2015/06/23/nine-cultural-value-differences-you-need-to-
know/#:~:text=Nine%20national%20cultural%20value%20differences%201%20Individualism
%20vs.,8%20Humane%20Orientation.%20...%209%20Indulgence%20vs.%20

Joshi, V. (2018). Entrepreneur. *The Importance of Having Diversity in the Workplace*.
Retrieved from, https://www.entrepreneur.com/article/322307

Litmos Heroes. (2014). How to Build Trust and Relationships. Retrieved from,
https://www.youtube.com/watch?v=wtNOq1Bwtt4

Liu, E., (2014). *How to Understand Power*. TED-Ed. Retrieved from,
https://www.youtube.com/watch?v=c_Eutci7ack

Loehr, A. (2016). *5 Tips to Managing Unconscious Bias at Work*. Retrieved from,
https://www.cornerstoneondemand.com/rework/5-tips-managing-unconscious-bias-work

Lumen. (n.d.). *Dimensions of Cultural Difference and their Effect*. Retrieved from,
https://courses.lumenlearning.com/wm-principlesofmanagement/chapter/dimensions-of-
cultural-difference-and-their-effect/

Mahdawi, A. (2016). *The Surprising Solution to Workplace Diversity*. TEDx Talks. Retrieved
from, https://www.youtube.com/watch?v=mtUlRYXJ0vI

Robbins, M. (2015). *Bring Your Whole Self to Work*. TEDxBerkeley. Retrieved from,
https://www.youtube.com/watch?v=bd2WKQWG_Dg

Robles, R. (2015). *Cultural Differences in Negotiation and Conflict*. Retrieved from, https://www.youtube.com/watch?v=rSDntIn6ekE

Rutledge, B. (2011). *Cultural Differences – The Power Distance Relationship*. Retrieved from, https://thearticulateceo.typepad.com/my-blog/2011/09/cultural-differences-the-power-distance-relationship.html

Sleeter, C. (2001). *Culture, Differences, & Power*. Retrieved from, http://www.edchange.org/multicultural/reviews/cd-sleeter.html

Speak First. (2009). *Cultural Diversity – Tips for Communicating with Cultural Diversity*. Retrieved from, https://www.youtube.com/watch?v=ZDvLk7e2Irc

UCSF. (n.d.). *Strategies to Address Unconscious Bias*. Retrieved from, https://diversity.ucsf.edu/resources/strategies-address-unconscious-bias

University of Texas - McCombs School of Business. (2018). *Implicit Bias | Concepts Unwrapped*. Retrieved from, https://www.youtube.com/watch?v=OoBvzI-YZf4

Index

[Created with **TExtract** /
    www.TExtract.com]

About the Author

Wesley E. Donahue, PhD, PE, PLS. PMP®, 6σ Black Belt

As a business owner, engineer, manager, and now an educator, I have traveled to over 24 countries and 49 states, helping other people succeed. But like you, at each step of the way I had to learn, and I had to put that learning into action. This workbook speaks from the voice of experience.

As for my background, I earned a B.S. in Engineering from Penn State University, an M.B.A. from Clarion University, a Ph.D. in Workforce Education from Penn State, and am a professor at Penn State. In this capacity, I am engaged in top-ranked graduate research and programing in learning and performance, lead a successful online graduate program in organization development and change, and teach education and engineering courses. I am also President of Centrestar, Inc., a firm that produces and delivers competency-based courses for professionals.

Before that, I was Director of Penn State Management Development Programs and Services. We provided education and training services to business and industry clients around the world. Prior to that, I had years of experience as a project manager, manager, and business owner. I was Regional Sales Vice President for Mark-Kay Plastics in Kansas City, Missouri; co-founder and Executive Vice President of Leffer Systems of New Jersey, a manufacturing company; and International Manager of Technology for Brockway, Inc., a Fortune 200 company. I also co-owned and operated a retail business for over ten years.

I am a registered professional engineer; professional land surveyor; six-sigma black belt; certified project management professional; co-author of *Creating In-house Sales Training and Development Programs;* and author of:

- *Building Leadership Competence: A Competency-Based Approach to Building Leadership Ability,*
- *Unlocking Lean Six Sigma: A Competency-Based Approach to Applying Continuous Process Improvement Principles and Best Practice,*
- *Professional Ethics: A Competency-Based Approach to Understanding and Appling Professional Ethics.*

I would enjoy hearing from you and learning how this workbook has helped you achieve your goals. Please contact me at wdonahue@centrestar.com

Best wishes for your continued success.

It is never too late to give up your prejudices.

- Henry David Thoreau

Made in United States
Troutdale, OR
04/19/2024

19238688R10051